# How To Solve Almost Any Sexual Problem The Easy Way

Tim Phizackerley

# Copyright and Disclaimer

ALL RIGHTS RESERVED. No part of this book may be reproduced or transmitted in any form whatsoever, electronic, or mechanical, including photocopying, recording, or by any informational storage or retrieval system without express written, dated and signed permission from the author.

DISCLAIMER AND/OR LEGAL NOTICES: The information presented herein represents the view of the author as of the date of publication. Because of the rate with which conditions change, the author reserves the right to alter and update his opinion based on the new conditions. The report is for informational purposes only.

While every attempt has been made to verify the information provided in this book, neither the author nor his affiliates/partners assume any responsibility for errors, inaccuracies or omissions. Any slights of people or organizations are unintentional.

If advice concerning medical or related matters is needed, the services of a fully qualified professional should be sought. This book is not intended for use as a source of medical advice. Any reference to any person or business whether living or dead is purely coincidental.

## TIM PHIZACKERLEY

Tim's consistent success in helping countless people find permanent relief from the pain and suffering caused by "poor programming" of the subconscious (including such severe and complex maladies as anorexia and bulimia) have motivated him to discovering new and improved tools and techniques that other therapists use as well as individuals use for self-help.

When conventional methods do not produce consistent results, Tim applies his knowledge and understanding of the subconscious toward development of effective strategies and tools to help people around the world finally experience true peace and joy in their lives.

Tim shares some of his perspectives about the human mind and finding solutions...

"Something which I have always been conscious of is that the human mind is the product of evolutionary processes. At its heart lies an organic computer. And the one thing which absolutely all computers have in common is that they run programs. As I delved deeper into the mechanisms underlying hypnosis I recognised certain things about the interaction between conscious and subconscious that I believed could open the door to literally reprogramming the subconscious computer in new and innovative ways."

In my work with clients I've been very systematic in finding solutions that work as efficiently as possible. I found that to do this one needs to have as good an understanding as possible of the ways in which people form concepts and process information. The upshot was that over the years I developed a fairly sophisticated model of the human mind and also the ways in which it processes and relates to information."

One of the truly groundbreaking and most effective tools and techniques that Tim will share with you in this book is Percussive Suggestion Technique or PSTEC. This revolutionary suite of tools covers the shift toward a more joyous, peaceful and positive subconscious that will support you in your desires and efforts to realize a more complete and wonderful life!

Immerse yourself because solutions are coming your way!

Visit:

www.pstec.org

This book is dedicated to the human race

# Contents

# Introduction

Sexual problems are common in both men and women so if you have one then you're by no means alone. The Journal of the American Medical Association reported that 43 percent of women surveyed indicated having sexual problems. A third of men surveyed also reported problems. The real figures are probably even higher especially since people tend not to want to share the fact they experience problems. Whatever the actual figures, the reality is that sexual problems are widespread. If you have a sexual problem of some kind then you're in good company because countless other people do too. While millions suffer in silence there may be no need because there are often relatively simple solutions and I'm going to describe as many as I can here.

This is a practical guide designed to help provide fast and effective help. This means that for most things, rather than getting bogged down in loads of theory I'm going to describe simple steps to rapid and effective solutions. To put this to work all you need to do is follow the steps.

Because so many sexual problems have similar causes and treatments, I originally had a lot of repetition in the text. In the end I decided that the format I've used here is the best and easiest to follow. I've split the information for you into chunks relating to certain things. In this way you'll have access to the information you need quickly and easily.

Where I explain a probable solution to any particular sexual problem you're likely to find that I've referred back to information in another section. This saves repetition and it's made this a much easier book for you to use than it would have been otherwise.

This approach to the subject also means you can focus on only those sections which apply to your specific issues. I do suggest reading everything cover to cover because you may find something in another section that's useful to you in an unexpected way.

For many people, sex is one of life's great pleasures. Sex can lift someone to great heights of fulfilment. Equally, sex and sexual difficulties can cause people to reach the depths of despair ... that is, if there's a significant problem. For many people, sex and sexuality can also be guilt and anxiety ridden, stressful, frustrating, painful, embarrassing or problematic in so many other ways.

This book is designed to help resolve as many sexual problems as possible. I'm going to describe simple, workable solutions that should work very well indeed as long as the instructions are followed.

Therapists can use these methods but I've deliberately produced this from a self-help perspective so you can help yourself. This is because I want to empower you with easy and effective solutions that stand a very high probability of working.

There's absolutely no point in being miserable when a solution exists and with this book you now have access to methods that can help with practically any sexual problem. If you have been dealing with something that isn't listed, read this cover to cover and you're likely to find information which you can use for whatever it is that you need to resolve.

I produced this book because so many people are simply too embarrassed to seek help for sexual problems. This is a tragedy because there are very often simple solutions and particularly so when it comes to subconscious or psychological problems related to sex.

Many people mistakenly assume that resolving such problems will be difficult. The reverse is true. Often the solution is likely to be reasonably simple as long as the correct approach is used. And the reality is that an extremely powerful tool already exists to help you. I'll be talking about it extensively and showing you how to use it to help yourself.

Wherever possible I'm also going to describe the simplest, fastest and most effective strategies to use. Levels of success may vary within particular time-scales but as you'll almost certainly discover, the methods and the tools described here will generally provide highly effective results and often extremely quickly.

I'm not telling you to use these methods. I can't do that. Since you'll be working to help yourself, you need to take responsibility for yourself and for the results you achieve.

Be very sure to follow the information carefully and also make sure that you have the downloadable tools you'll need. Once you have the self-help tools I'm about to describe, you can simply refer to the sections for whatever problem needs to be dealt with and work through the steps.

If you have more than one sexual problem to resolve then I suggest working on them one at a time. Once you're satisfied with the result then that's the correct time to move onto the next.

Just in case you're unfamiliar with me, perhaps I should introduce myself.
I'm a therapist and also an expert on hypnosis and the subconscious. I've created a wide variety of therapeutic interventions that are being used all around the World with tremendous success. The focus of my work has always been on providing the fastest, easiest and most effective solutions available anywhere.

# PSTEC

In order to provide fast and effective solutions, this book is going to introduce you to something called PSTEC. You may already know about it.

PSTEC is short for Percussive Suggestion Technique. It's an extremely powerful and highly effective therapy and self-improvement tool. It's designed for effective use on almost any psychological problem or solution. It has uses beyond that too. PSTEC has a growing worldwide reputation for working very well and very fast. You can use it in the privacy of your own home to resolve almost any psychological problem. It's highly effective and it's been endorsed as such by countless therapists and thousands of self-helpers.

PSTEC is in use around the world amongst English speakers and is also being translated into a number of other languages. As more and more people discover the power of PSTEC, it's gathering ever more enthusiastic users and supporters every day. PSTEC can also help you with things such as phobias, fears, anxiety and stress. PSTEC is a set of tools which is completely modular and very flexible. It's designed to create conscious and subconscious change...fast....very fast!

If you search the Internet you'll find that people all over the world have endorsed it for three reasons. These are speed, ease of use and sheer effectiveness.
It was created in order to make personal change as easy, effortless, effective and as fast as it can be. It works on the subconscious in ways which are difficult to describe until you experience them for yourself. Most people are amazed.

The reason I'm well qualified to explain how to use this tool is because I'm the therapist who invented, designed and created it. This gives me a unique understanding as to its capabilities. Another reason why I wanted to create this guide is because your life should be as good as it can be.

# Action:
# First download the 100% free PSTEC therapy system.

PSTEC is a modular system for creating change at the level of the subconscious. It comes in the form of audio downloads. The basic system is completely free. You can use the basic system to change emotional responses to experiences, thoughts and imagined events. This means you can use the basic system to resolve a truly mind boggling range of problems and usually it will work on them all.

There is an International Register of PSTEC Therapists and also a free forum.

So begin by downloading the free system. Remember to join the mailing list too because you will get free notifications, access to the latest information, interviews with real users of PSTEC and also lots of other useful hints and tips.

PSTEC has a variety of tools available and I'll explain what they are in a moment.

Within the PSTEC range of tools there are free tools and there are also tools that you can buy. I'll talk about both in this book. Even though I'll talk about both I'm going to ensure that you can use this book with just the free tools if needs be. If you read the section called "Understanding the PSTEC Tools" you'll find information about this.

You can download the free PSTEC therapy system at:

http://www.pstec.org
or
http://www.pstecaudiosource.org

# Types of Sexual Problems

There are essentially two basic types of sexual problem. There are physical problems and there are psychological ones. There are also problems which are a combination of both. Where a physical problem exists it is likely to have affected you in some way psychologically. This might be worries and concerns or frustration for example.

When it comes to sexual problems, sometimes the same or similar symptoms can have more than one possible cause and therefore it can also have more than one possible approach to treatment.

Where a problem might be physical in nature it makes sense to get checked out by a doctor. Once medical reasons have been eliminated the alternative is that something subconscious is at work. Some people worry that if they have a problem which is psychological in origin their mind must not be working properly. Fortunately, that's total nonsense. A brain which is working perfectly sometimes does unexpected things for reasons which I will explore later.

Psychological problems can happen to absolutely anyone. They are very common and as you'll see later in this book, a psychological problem very often isn't a problem at all. It's more like something else which is waiting for a better solution to be applied.

The self-help tools and methods I'm going to describe provide the means to successfully treat a huge variety of psychological problems. They can even also be used to help you cope with physical problems.

Sexual problems which originate in the mind are called psycho-sexual. It's not a term I'll use much because I like to keep things simple and very readable.

It's important to remember that even a psycho-sexual problem can have real physical symptoms. Just because a problem seems to be physical in nature, it doesn't necessarily mean it's a medical problem.

Psychological reasons VERY often underpin sexual problems with physical symptoms. A lack of sufficient vaginal lubrication is a good example and non-organic erectile dysfunction is another.

Sexual problems which originate in the mind are extremely common, and it's primarily for those kinds of issues that this book has been created. Problems with psychological causes are also often very easy to resolve with the right methods. As I've indicated already though, psychological tools and methods can also help you deal very well with something which is physical.

The techniques and methods you're going to learn are as simple as I can make them and will generally be extremely effective.

## Sex as an Indicator of Physical Health

Some physical problems connected with sex may indicate undiagnosed health problems, and sometimes even quite serious ones, so a discussion with your doctor may well be advisable. Where appropriate I've tried to indicate this.

# Subconscious Essentials

Your subconscious mind powerfully affects your sex life and your sexuality.

Few people would consciously decide to ruin their sex lives by having sexual problems. And even if they did they'd be unlikely to be reading this book. Psychological problems related to sex tend to be a kind of subconscious "sexual sabotage." But it's sabotage for a reason and there is ALWAYS a reason.

Sometimes the reasons for such "sabotage" may be obvious but usually they are not and especially so to the person concerned. For example, if you're stuck in a loveless marriage then your subconscious may have made decisions about the benefits of allowing you to enjoy a normal sex life in that environment.

If the marriage is abusive then a woman might not want a child brought up in those surroundings. Whatever the reasons for it happening, a person's subconscious can "throw a spanner in the works" for any one of a multitude of reasons.

Some people incorrectly regard their subconscious as being either non-existent or a non-important aspect of themselves. They've heard the word but it's just some vague concept and they think it doesn't really make any difference to them or their lives.

Other people regard their subconscious almost as though it were another person outside of their influence and none of their responsibility.

In both cases nothing could be further from the truth. In reality your subconscious is very real and it's also very much a part of you. In fact it's the essence of who you are because every emotion you ever had comes from your subconscious.

For this and several other reasons, it's very important to realise that what you choose to allow yourself to think consciously does affect what your subconscious does for you. And where there isn't a physical or a medical reason for a sexual problem then successful treatment will almost always rely on helping your subconscious to solve the problem for you. You see it's your subconscious that decides what physical responses are appropriate and when. Blushing is a really good example of something where the subconscious controls a physical response.

For some women sex can be difficult because of muscle spasms, vaginal dryness, pain or failure to climax for some other reason. And for some men getting and maintaining an erection may be difficult despite hundreds of millions of years of evolution working to create a system which works perfectly. And what about having an erection long enough to share some mutual enjoyment before ejaculating?

Even simple problems can cause someone to feel inadequate and it can impact on self-confidence and on relationships in so many ways.

Different people with different sexual problems may have those problems because of subconscious intervention and may even have identical causes. Identical causes can result in a variety of symptoms. Conversely there could be tens of thousands of people with different causes but exactly the same symptoms. This means that finding a solution is likely to require several steps and some experimentation but not always.

One thing's for sure. If your subconscious seems to be making sex problematic then there's always a reason for that. So from a treatment perspective it's important to deal with whatever reasons there might be for your subconscious mind to do what it's been doing.

I've been using hypnosis to find the causes of subconscious problems for many years. Often I do this by hypnotically regressing people to past experiences. I've been able to identify the exact causes of countless otherwise mysterious problems in this way and after I've done this, usually it's been a relatively simple matter to remove the causes and correct their problem.

But if you're doing self-help how can you do this? Well I'm not going to suggest that you should even try because I don't rate your chances of regressing yourself. Fortunately there are certain things which occur very commonly and which could very well be the cause of problems when it comes to sex. So in this book I suggest as many likely candidates as possible.

If you want the nearest equivalent to being able to hypnotically regress yourself refer to the section on PSTEC Accelerators.

Some key points:

- Your subconscious mind works as a guardian to protect you.
- Your subconscious is very flexible and it can often resolve problems very quickly if dealt with appropriately.
- Your subconscious is where all your emotions come from.
- It doesn't like negative or painful emotions and your subconscious will sometimes take steps to avoid them.
- Despite this, your subconscious may sometimes use painful emotions as the means to direct conscious action.
- Your subconscious is real!

## A problem is not always a problem

Your subconscious mind identifies problems and very often it silently puts solutions in place for you. This is a system which works brilliantly most of the time so it's something to be grateful for.

But occasionally the subconscious will do something which seems less than useful. And this means that much of what we experience consciously as problems, are not problems at all. Often a sexual problem is actually a subconsciously designed and implemented solution for something else.

You see, the subconscious mind has a tendency to find solutions to what it perceives as a problem but it doesn't tell you. Very often to our conscious minds those "solutions" can seem more like problems of their own. And if your life has not been going to plan in the "bedroom department" and there's no medical reason as to why, then there's got to be a reason somewhere. After medical reasons have been eliminated there's really only one other place to look, and that's at your Subconscious.

If a problem is not medical in origin then it almost certainly has a subconscious cause and it's likely that your subconscious has almost certainly been misguidedly doing its best so now is the time to help it out.

Every expert on the subconscious seems to agree that your subconscious works as a guardian and protector and it's very often in this capacity that it takes action. I've seen the results of this guardian aspect of the subconscious in my own therapy clients countless times, and not just related to sexual problems.

Take the example of a dog phobia. No one wants to have a phobia because a phobia is a really unpleasant thing to live with. But let's suppose someone was bitten by a dog when they were four years old. What can their subconscious do to protect them? The guardian part of the subconscious mind in its role as protector decides that it MUST protect them from that ever happening again so it takes steps. The guardian part of the subconscious has limited control over conscious decision making but it wants to keep that person away from dogs so there can't be a repeat of them getting bitten. So to fix this their subconscious creates a powerful fear of dogs.

The subconscious mind knows very well that with an overpowering fear in place that person will tend to avoid dogs. This avoidance keeps them away from dogs as much as possible and this helps to keep them "safe". Consciously that person wishes that they didn't have a dog phobia at all because they don't like it, but subconsciously the fear makes complete sense because it helps to prevent them being bitten again.

The same applies to many sexual problems. Consciously the person will usually wish there wasn't a problem but subconsciously that problem exists for a reason. So what about sex and how can the subconscious affect that? Well, for one thing you've almost certainly got very little or no direct conscious control over the way your muscles react during sex or to natural lubrication, erections or the exact moment of orgasm. That's also unconsciously controlled. And what about the ability to have an orgasm at all? You need to realise that your subconscious mind has a powerful influence over all of these things and much more besides.

Your subconscious mind may seem totally inaccessible but it's every bit as much a part of you as your heart or liver. You don't see those either but they work in the background to help you and so does your subconscious. In fact your subconscious mind has some very specific and extremely important functions and it does its job to the best of its ability.

As I've already mentioned, your subconscious tries hard to work as a guardian for you. Because of its guardian function it will generally try to protect you from any danger but crucially those dangers may be real or imagined and imagined dangers are based on experience.

This means that past experience and also what you do with your conscious thoughts and with your imagination can have a very powerful effect on what your subconscious does or doesn't do for you.

In reality your subconscious mind should be your very best friend because it has the power to resolve so much if you simply give it the chance and the right encouragement. It absolutely definitely has the ability to resolve a great many sexual problems because very often it created them in the first place.

It's because of your subconscious that I suggest you use PSTEC.

The PSTEC tools are all designed to create subconscious changes quickly, easily and powerfully. Because so many sexual problems are subconscious in origin, this is exactly why PSTEC can be so incredibly useful in resolving sexual problems. PSTEC tools change the way your subconscious behaves and reacts. PSTEC can remove fears and worries totally. PSTEC can resolve guilt if that is an issue. It can also be used to re-educate your subconscious and give it understanding of things which you'd hope it would know. PSTEC tools can change subconscious reactions and behaviours. PSTEC can also be used to suggest new ways of doing things for your subconscious to follow. When it comes to the subconscious there's little that can't be done with PSTEC and in the next section I'll explain the elements of PSTEC, including the Click Tracks and also PSTEC Positive.

If you're unfamiliar with PSTEC then the above names may sound very strange indeed but rest assured you'll soon get used to them. It's all pretty easy and if you're unfamiliar with just how powerful and effective the PSTEC tools are then you're probably in for a major and very pleasant surprise.

# Understanding
# the PSTEC Tools

There are more tools within the PSTEC stable than I'm about to list here. Here are some of the most commonly used ones.

## 1) PSTEC Click Tracks

PSTEC comes to you in the form of a downloadable therapy system. Hopefully you already have the MP3 files for the free PSTEC therapy system but if not then you should go get them immediately. The free system is genuinely free and won't cost you a dime. It's way more powerful than you probably expect so do go get it.

Just visit www.pstec.org or www.pstecaudiosource.org and download the free system.

The free PSTEC therapy system contains some extremely powerful self-help tools called Click Tracks. You can use the Click Tracks for dealing with any negative emotions of any kind. Those emotions may be related to something in the past, the present, or to something upcoming or imagined in the future. The purpose of the Click Tracks is that they can very quickly neutralise even the most powerful negative emotions and they work with tremendous effectiveness and reliability.

Hint: Be absolutely sure to follow the instructions to the letter in order to get them to work at their very best.

## 2) Enhanced Effectiveness Click Tracks (EEfs)

In addition to the free Click Tracks which are used to neutralise unwanted negative emotions, there are some even more powerful versions. These are called EEfs which is short for Enhanced Effectiveness Click Tracks (EEfs). These are designed for neutralising powerful negative emotions too.

They are supplied as part of something called PSTEC Level 1. The EEfs work exactly like the free Click Tracks but they also contain special enhancements. The free Click Tracks will clear most emotionally related things but if you need them the EEfs are another step up in power. They also provide useful variety.

You can use EEfs for neutralising any negative emotions. Those emotions may be related to something in the past, in the present, or to something upcoming or imagined in the future.

If I refer to Click Tracks later I also mean that you can use EEfs if you have them.

## 3) PSTEC Positive

The simplest way to think of PSTEC Positive is as a tremendously effective delivery mechanism for any suggestion of change to your subconscious mind.
PSTEC Positive is rather like using an affirmation but with an awesome super power and energy behind it.

PSTEC Positive is NOT designed to change emotions. Use PSTEC Click Tracks, EEfs or Accelerators for that.

PSTEC Positive is very commonly used for changing beliefs.

You can also use PSTEC Positive to change perceptions about experiences, past or future.

And PSTEC Positive can be used to suggest new habits and actions to your subconscious.

PSTEC Positive can be used to change behaviours and very often this is done in a direct way, but you can also change behaviours in an indirect way. By which I mean that subconsciously generated behaviour can be changed by suggesting a new behaviour to your subconscious or instead by changing the beliefs which created those behaviours in the first place. So if the direct approach doesn't work for any reason, indirect methods are likely to be needed instead.

There are two types of PSTEC Positive. One form of PSTEC Positive requires tapping and the other doesn't. The instructions for both are included with the tracks.

Both versions of PSTEC Positive are slightly different in terms of how you use them. Unless otherwise stated, the advice given in this guide applies equally to both types.

PSTEC Positive is an optional extra with PSTEC.

**If you don't have PSTEC Positive then you can substitute the use of affirmations and positive self-talk. The reason that you should use PSTEC Positive rather than affirmations is because even a single use of PSTEC**

**Positive is equal to a few hundred affirmations.**

For anyone with a genuine interest in getting the most from PSTEC and the Click Tracks, then PSTEC Level 1 is an excellent start. PSTEC Positive comes as part of PSTEC Level 1 along with lots more goodies and detailed tutorials. This is to allow you to resolve a huge variety of personal issues and problems, not just sexual ones.

# 4) The PSTEC Accelerators

Accelerators are another optional extra and have more than one function. PSTEC works very quickly but accelerators make PSTEC work even faster and even more powerful. If you decide to use accelerators then they can also be used to help you remember causal memories and this can be useful in order to make your self-help work easier and more successful.

The Accelerators come with a tutorial which explains exactly how to use them. There are two types of Accelerator. There are two relaxation type Accelerators and two tapping type Accelerators.

The PSTEC Accelerators (tapping type) are used exactly like the free Click Tracks but they are yet another step up in power. They contain even more powerful enhancements and they will often shift issues that nothing else could. More than that, the Accelerators contain special suggestions designed to speed your progress with ALL other PSTEC products and tools.

You can use PSTEC Accelerators alongside the other core tracks such as the Click Tracks, and you can also make use of them with things like weight loss, the PSTEC smoking cessation system and even my totally free package for anyone with cancer.

You can use Accelerators for dealing with any negative emotions. Those emotions may be related to something in the past, something in the present, or perhaps to something upcoming or imagined in the future.

The tapping Accelerators can also be used like the tapping version of PSTEC Positive. This is not commonly done, but it is a feature of the Accelerators (tapping type) that they can be used in that way.

## 5) "PSTEC for Stress in the Moment"

"PSTEC for Stress in the Moment" may be useful in this context. It is another optional PSTEC tool. It allows you to pre-programme your subconscious so that if something stressful occurs at any time, then your subconscious will automatically know how to deal with it and help you to stay calm.

You can also call on it consciously at a moment's notice if you ever need to. This is done by mentally reaching up and imagining that you flick a switch to switch off stress in your mind. The result? Instant genuine calm.

Think of "PSTEC for Stress in the Moment" as being rather like a capacitor or rechargeable battery. You listen to this track and follow its instructions in order to charge up your internal battery with calm. Then when needed you can automatically release that calmness and stress handling capability to deal with anything that crops up in your life.

If sex is stressful or if you think it might be then "PSTEC for Stress in the Moment" may be a good tool for you to explore. Most people who have used it seem to agree that it works almost like a magic wand.

## 6) Click Tracks Made Simple

The truly wonderful Jeff Harding and I put together an introduction to PSTEC and understanding the many ways it can totally transform your life. The tutorial is called "Click Tracks Made Simple". If you have a willingness to share your discovery of PSTEC through Facebook you can access it completely for free.

For details visit www.pstec.org or www.pstecaudiosource.org

# Fear of Seeing Your Doctor

Some sexual problems can be indicators of health problems so a visit to the doctor to discuss the situation will often be advisable. Ultimately the responsibility for the decision as to whether you see a doctor is yours, but at the very least I can suggest it to you as often being a good idea.

As an example let's assume that a medical problem is the cause of a sexual problem you wish to deal with. It could be painful intercourse or erectile dysfunction for example. To see the problem resolved a visit to the doctor might be an essential step but so many people choose not to do this for fear of embarrassment. As such they may miss perhaps a very simple solution to the problem. That makes no sense at all. Please get seen because it may be that the problem is easily resolved by means of a simple intervention. It could also be that the reason for the problem is because of an underlying health problem so it makes sense to have a discussion with a doctor.

If the prospect of discussing your sex life with your doctor fills you with fear, embarrassment or dread then you may decide to explore psychological solutions first. Personally I strongly advise most things be discussed with a doctor just to be sure.

If you're putting off seeing a doctor because of embarrassment or fear then this is the first way that you can use PSTEC Click Tracks. If you use the free Click Tracks they will usually eliminate any such fears and feelings of embarrassment with ease.

That will allow you to see your doctor with confidence and get the medical side of things checked out.

.

# Common Causes
# of Sexual Problems

Sexual problems have two common origins: Medical or physical causes and subconscious or psychological causes. I'm going to leave your doctor to deal with medical diagnoses but I will highlight a few things for you where appropriate.

My own expertise is in the domain of the subconscious. Where sexual problems do exist, very often it can be that the subconscious is actually sabotaging normal sexual function. By creating subconscious changes such problems can very often be easily and quite quickly resolved.

It can be helpful to realise that the subconscious works much like a computer. Your subconscious does it's best to identify problems and then create solutions. Unfortunately its solutions can be rather unwanted and frustrating to our conscious way of looking at things.

The problem of course is that subconscious actions happen outside of conscious control and this means that you're left with the result of your subconscious actions but no conscious idea as to the reason.

If only you knew why your subconscious does the things it does, then you could perhaps help it to find a better solution. Often, just giving the subconscious some new and useful information will solve a problem, sexual or otherwise. This is true even if that problem has existed all your adult life or longer. The PSTEC tools allow you to do this in several ways.

If you had conscious access to all the reasons for all the things your subconscious has been doing then that would be ideal. Working with a skilled therapist like myself, it's often possible to access the subconscious in a very direct way and to discover the exact reasons for any problems. But when you're doing self-help it can sometimes be difficult to identify a very specific cause and very often it is easier to consider all the likely possible subconscious reasons for any given sexual problem. Then you apply my suggested solutions to all of those things.

Here's a very important question:

"Have you had any experiences which might have made some part of your subconscious want to avoid sex or to be less than enthusiastic about it?"

If you can answer that question then you'll already be half way to a solution and there are lots of things that commonly turn up as reasons for sexual problems. I'm going to share some of the commonest so you can explore them.

For example, if you're a woman have you ever had an abortion? Or if you're man have you ever been the father of an aborted child? Abortions tend to affect women more deeply than men because they are so much more directly involved but men can be affected too. Many women have abortions and huge numbers of women find the entire experience extremely distressing. For most women the decision to terminate a pregnancy is a hard one and the experience can be emotionally scarring.

Commonly there are ongoing feelings and beliefs associated with having had an abortion. Very often there is deep rooted guilt attached. Sometimes there is anger towards oneself or towards someone else. There can also be great sadness and grief attached to abortions. Abortions are far more than the physical experience and for many women the emotional consequences persist consciously and subconsciously, for a lifetime.

If this has been the case then this might be reason enough for the subconscious to have taken steps to reduce the chances of the same thing happening again. Making sex difficult and less appealing reduces the chance of an abortion in the future. This is one common example of the guardian aspect of the subconscious at work.

In hypnotic regression and analysis the subconscious mind often yields information regarding its actions. Abortions very frequently show up as causing problems. These problems don't just relate to sex. Abortions can also be related to such things as eating disorders, OCD, and problems with feelings of low self-worth. For this reason I strongly advise that guilt, anger, grief or sadness connected with an abortion be cleared using the PSTEC Click Tracks.

Remember that the Click Tracks are able to neutralise such emotions. Doing this allows your subconscious to behave differently.

With the advent of contraception it is easier for most women to avoid unwanted pregnancy than it ever has been. Because precautions are available but not always used this can be another reason why people often feel so terribly guilty about having had an abortion. Clearing the heavy guilt or fear connected with having had an abortion in the past may well be more than enough to get a sex life back on track.

Along similar lines, you should also clear any negative emotions attached to miscarriages. That could be feelings of grief, guilt, fear, and so on. Such feelings vary person to person.

Other things to examine and clear using the PSTEC Click Tracks are:

1. Unpleasant sexual experiences of the past,
2. Fears or anxiety related to pregnancy,
3. Fear or anxiety related to child birth, or becoming a parent,
4. Anxiety about contraception,
5. Anger towards a partner,
6. Anxiety about sex itself,
7. Guilt regarding sex and sexual expression,
8. Fear or anxiety about showing your body,
9. Anything else that might cause concern regarding sex.

My advice is to use the PSTEC Click Tracks to clear those emotions if they do exist.

It's important to use Click Tracks to remove any and all negative emotions attached to these kinds of things because any or all of these could provide sufficient reasons for your subconscious to introduce roadblocks to a full and enjoyable sex life.

In other words, examine your emotions towards sex and sexual expression. If there's a negative emotion there, either in the present or in your past, then use Click Tracks to eliminate those negative feelings. This will change your subconscious response at some level and it may be all it takes to resolve many sexual problems.

Along similar lines you should also look at your beliefs regarding yourself and sex. For example do you have any of the following beliefs?

1) The thought or belief that sex is wrong or dirty
2) Negative beliefs regarding sexual pleasure
2) Beliefs that you do not enjoy sex
4) Negative beliefs regarding your abilities as a lover
5) The belief that wanting sex is incompatible with being a decent person or a good person
6) That you don't deserve sexual fulfilment
7) Were you brought up with strong religious objections to sexual expression?

If you want a happy and trouble free sex life then for maximum success, these beliefs and ALL similar beliefs are best dealt with if they exist. If you do not remove them or at least change them then they are likely to create conflicts within you.

PSTEC Positive is the tool to use to change your beliefs, consciously and also subconsciously. You can also make use of your self-talk.

Let's suppose you've believed that sex is wrong or sex is dirty. Well there must be a reason for such beliefs if they do exist in you. Your parents might even have brought you up to feel that way.

Well if you have such a belief, or if one was instilled in you, then sex or wanting sex is likely to create anxiety because of the internal conflict. (Desire being in conflict with belief) The anxiety created by the conflict can in turn create sexual dysfunction and sexual problems.

To avoid this you would need to undertake to deliberately change any such beliefs. The basic method is to choose to deliberately hold a belief which does NOT cause such an internal conflict. No conflict = no anxiety. With the anxiety gone, the guardian part of the subconscious no longer needs to use protective mechanisms to interfere with sex and all can be as it should be.

Fortunately, PSTEC Positive can be used to create changes to beliefs. This applies to those you hold consciously and also subconsciously.

**Remember that affirmations can be used as an alternative but for most people, affirmations are hundreds of times weaker than PSTEC positive.**

If you have the belief that sex is wrong or dirty and want to avoid anxiety connected with that kind of belief then you MUST change your beliefs about sex being that way. There is an alternative but I don't recommend it if you want to avoid subconscious problems. The alternative is to exploit any rebellious streak and to delight in doing something bad or dirty and some people do this but generally suffer indirect consequences as a result. By preference I strongly advise you to eliminate any belief that sex is wrong or dirty instead.

If you do want a trouble free sex life then it's best to have the belief that sex is perfectly natural, good for you and also totally normal. This kind of belief does not create anxiety. Instead these are beliefs which are 100% conducive to relaxation, normal function and pleasure when having sex. If trying to resolve sexual problems this is the kind of belief to generate within yourself if not there already. Your subconscious will thank you for it!

Deliberately changing your beliefs (conscious and subconscious) requires a choice to be made and a change in thinking and self-talk. You inform your subconscious by using PSTEC Positive, but ONLY do this after using the Click Tracks on any pre-existing or associated anxiety.

After clearing any anxiety with Click Tracks you can use PSTEC Positive to suggest beliefs to your subconscious mind in order for the anxiety to not be created in the first place.

Here are some examples of the kinds of suggestions that you might choose to use in this instance:

*Sex is natural*
*Sex is good for me*
*I can relax about sex now*
*Now I'm an adult sex is good for me*
*I will always have safe sex*
*Sex is important and healthy*
*I love my wife and I want to please her*
*I love husband and I want to please him*
*Sex makes me a better (father or mother)*

For sex to work well you want the beliefs that sex is normal, perfectly natural and good for you. In other words you want your mind and particularly your subconscious mind to be able to relax and really go with it.

## Beliefs

Your beliefs came from somewhere and you haven't always had them. As children we are heavily influenced by parents and peers. Between them they can set our beliefs in very specific directions.

Your beliefs and attitudes towards sex will also have come from observation and experience.

Common factors:
When you were young, who were the first people you knew were having sex?
If it was other youngsters, did you like them? If you didn't like them then you may have spent your whole life unconsciously avoiding being like them. If you think that's a factor then as soon as you

become consciously aware of it, any subconscious effect it had on you will be weakened. You can Click Track that dislike of course.

What about the seamier side of sex?
What are your feelings about pornography, prostitution, strip clubs, rape, rent boys, singers, dogging, sex scandals etc?

You hold beliefs about all those things and for many people beliefs do have the effect of making sex and sexuality seem bad or wrong at some level. Perhaps those things seem base or animalistic to you. And even if you consciously don't feel that way, there's likely to be a part of you which does.

You see, whatever your physical age, mentally you exist at many other ages too. If you're 45 or 50 years old then there's still a part of you which is 20years old, and another part of your mind which is 10 years, 5 years, or 3 years old because the neural programs which you laid down at those times are still operating ... At least to an extent.

Often when looking to resolve problems you may need to examine and perhaps change beliefs. This is because your emotions and feelings are very heavily dependent upon them. Beliefs can affect you physically and sexually in ways you may not be aware of or have ever considered.

Take the example of beliefs related to sex outside of marriage. A woman who believes that sex outside of marriage is totally wrong, or who was brought up to believe that, is very likely to feel very guilty and anxious if she actually has sex outside of marriage. For this particular woman, with those beliefs, even wanting sex in this way would create a massive conflict within her. As a rule, internal conflicts are bad. They create anxiety and anxiety can create problems.

But another woman may have entirely different beliefs. She may have been brought up to believe that it makes absolute sense for a woman to be able to enjoy all the sex she likes whether inside or outside of marriage. With that belief set she will not be troubled by guilt at all. She has great sex, lots of it, and there is no conflict.

Here's why this is so important. Your emotions are usually a consequence of the beliefs you hold. Beliefs affect your emotions very powerfully. Some beliefs cause wide ranging negative emotions and conflicts. Emotions and particularly negative ones such as fear, guilt and anger can powerfully affect your subconscious and in turn they can affect your physical responses.

If your beliefs seem not to be working for you in a positive or useful way, then it's time to stop and think. Carefully consider whether those are beliefs you genuinely want to have. It can also be useful to consider where your beliefs came from and sometimes you may need to carefully evaluate what your beliefs are doing for you. For this reason, it's often the case that beliefs MUST be changed to see a result. Your beliefs have real life consequences because your beliefs affect your emotions, your subconscious, your physical responses and also your physiology.

## Expectations

It's important to recognise that your expectations can also powerfully affect your physical body and what it does.

You'll be familiar with the concepts of mind and body. In reality the whole idea of a mind and a body is a total nonsense. Your mind and your body are both part of the exactly same thing ... you.

The computer in your car or television is part of the car or telly. You don't talk about those things as being different. The very idea of mind and body as separate things is an artificial distinction and it's often not a helpful one. The reality is that by doing things differently in your mind, your body will respond. This is because mind and body are both parts of the same system. This interrelatedness is why mental stress affects people physically.

This simple principle means that any mental change can powerfully affect your physical responses including sexual ones and your expectations powerfully affect your body's responses. If you're a woman and you genuinely and fully expect your vagina to relax and open and to be well lubricated ready for pleasurable sex then there's an excellent chance that it will do that. And if you're a man and fully expect that an erection is going to happen every time you want one then it's very likely to be the case.

By contrast if you continually expect problems then that's what you're likely to experience because your subconscious will work to make it a reality.

Fortunately, as well as using PSTEC Positive to change your beliefs, you can also use it to change your expectations. This is because expectations are actually beliefs. Expectations are simply beliefs about the future.
This means that you can decide what expectation you want to have and then use PSTEC Positive to build it.

Remember that using PSTEC Positive is rather like asking a skilled hypnotist to make something real in your mind. PSTEC Positive is very different from hypnosis but it does the job of delivering your chosen suggestions to your subconscious. The result? Change! The greater the amount of use, the greater the change.

You will find instructions on exactly how to use PSTEC Positive along with the tracks themselves. There's also more information about PSTEC Positive in the section on PSTEC.

Lastly I want to say something about doubts. Genuinely buying into an expectation is not the same thing as just telling yourself something and at the same time hanging on to doubt.

When it comes to undertaking any personal change, one of the best things that you can do is eliminate doubt as much as possible. Wherever there is doubt there is a contradictory belief or expectation. If you think of expectations as being instructions for your subconscious to follow then you need to send clear ones. Doubts send an opposing instruction to the one you genuinely want the subconscious to process.

You can use PSTEC Positive to help eliminate doubts. The way to do this is simple: Choose suggestions which reinforce the positive expectation you want to create. The more you reinforce an expectation the more you eliminate doubt.

## Self-image

Self-image and sexual problems may be connected. Certain sections of this book mention self-image as being an important consideration and factor. Rather than go into details of every one of those here I will mention it only in the appropriate sections.

Some sections in this book will advise that you may need to work on your self-image in order to get full resolution of certain sexual problems. The need to do this may not be immediately obvious in some cases which is why I will discuss it where appropriate. The simplest way to improve self-image is by getting into the habit of using more positive self-talk. This is hard for many people though because they simply don't feel that way. Under those circumstances any positive self-talk will be almost immediately countered with something negative, also said internally.

For most people, positive thinking simply doesn't work unless certain steps precede it. When you are negatively emotional about something it is hard to impact on the belief structure which creates those feelings while they exist.

**Therefore, the first step is to change your emotional state in that regard.**

This is done by applying Click Tracks to that negative emotion in order to reduce it. You can use the free PSTEC therapy system to do that. Alternatively you can use PSTEC EEfs or accelerators if you have them. No matter how you reduce the negative feelings you may have towards yourself you do need to lower that emotion as a first step.

It is only after doing this that you can really begin effective work on the network of beliefs which made you feel that way about yourself.

Beliefs can be changed by identifying them and then deliberately making changes. (See also the section on Beliefs)

The first and most important step is simply to cultivate the habit of changing your self-talk so that it's more positive and empowering than it has been.
What kinds of things should you be saying to yourself as a matter of habit?
If you don't know, then here's my suggested way of finding out.

Consider that your parents or guardians and other significant people essentially programmed you when you were young. Their words will have created many of your initial beliefs about self. What kinds of things would you have wanted your parents to have been saying to you on a daily basis? What positive and empowering things could they have told you over and over that would have created a better self-image?

As an adult you have the opportunity to be saying those things to yourself. Undertake to use your self-talk to create those beliefs which will benefit and empower you but remember that you will need to use Click Tracks first in order to remove any strong negative emotions about those beliefs.

If you want more help with this then you may wish to explore "PSTEC Level 1" and also "PSTEC Positive Secrets". Both are available on www.pstec.org and also at www.pstecaudiosource.org

## Stress

Stress can affect you sexually and in lots of other ways. Stress comes in more than one flavour. There are short term stresses and there can be longer more protracted periods of stress. They are different and affect us differently. They also need to be dealt with differently.

PSTEC Click Tracks provide a quick and easy means to deal with the things that are immediately stressful in your life. You can also use them to deal with the lingering stressful impact of bad things that have happened in the past. (See section on PSTEC and the Click Tracks)

Sometimes though, life throws one thing after another at you. In fact it can sometimes seem to send an ongoing stream of stressful factors resulting in long and more protracted periods of stress.

A serious disagreement with an employer or a period of bullying is a classic example of a longer term stress causing event. Our own family is no stranger to stress so I understand this very well. For example my wife has been terminally ill twice and has also waited for and has also undergone three organ transplants.

If stress is ongoing then I highly recommend that you use the PSTEC tool "Stress In The Moment". It's mostly designed for dealing with unexpected stresses but is also absolutely ideal for dealing with long periods of stress.
Remember to use the Click Tracks too of course for anything specific.

Another thing that you should do with long term stress is to look carefully at your eating habits. If you are eating or drinking lots of very unhealthy, sugar or caffeine loaded products then a change in your diet to remove them will help you too.

So take a look at the food you eat and if there is anything like this which seems like a compulsion then you should eradicate it. Obviously few people know how to do this for themselves and this is why I created the PSTEC "Food and Drink Compulsion Breakers". The PSTEC "Food and Drink Compulsion Breakers" seem to be nearly bullet proof in shifting such problems.

The food and drink compulsion breakers are designed to switch off any food compulsion for junk food or drink in a matter of minutes, and for those results to last long term.

Since releasing these tracks lots of people have told me that they are now experiencing long periods of calm whereas they were not before simply because of the rubbish they were eating. They've also told me that those tracks have worked for them on every junk food they've directed them at. As a consequence they are feeling totally different about themselves. They're losing weight, eating well, feeling good about themselves and crucially they feel less stressed because they are not suffering the chemical assault on their minds and bodies that they were before.

Certainly if you are undergoing long term stress then do look at the food you eat. If it is loaded with sugar and caffeine (e.g. colas) especially, then a change is likely to help you a lot. If you struggle to stop eating junk then these tracks can help you rid yourself of any junk food compulsion.

Earlier I said that sometimes life can *seem* to send an ongoing stream of stressful factors your way. I chose those words carefully because "seem" is the crucial word to notice here. Often something that would be highly stressful for one person is not stressful for another and the significant difference between two such people is the beliefs that they hold.

Let's suppose that a business suffers a disaster. Under such circumstances one business owner might feel hugely stressed because they're focussed on catastrophe and constantly tell themselves there is absolutely no way out.

Another business owner will see it simply as a setback which requires a solution to be found. They'll also tell themselves that they'll find the solution and that the business will be ten times better afterwards.

One of these people is likely to feel massively stressed but the other is not. A deliberate change in attitude can work absolute wonders for your stress levels. (See the section on Beliefs)

## Assistance or more information

PSTEC has a forum so you can bounce ideas off other people. Sharing experiences can be helpful for all. If you would rather not discuss sexual issues but need help working out exactly how to frame suggestions in the most powerful way, then there is a detailed tutorial available called "Success with PSTEC and PSTEC Positive."

If you discuss things with your partner you can also bounce ideas around and this may be very useful.

PSTEC is something you can explore minimally or fully. I suggest you explore it fully because you can use it for almost anything. Here I'm keeping things as simple as possible, but if you want in depth knowledge then the information is readily available via the various PSTEC tutorials.

# Anorgasmia, Vaginismus & Dysparenuia

Let's begin with three of the commonest sexual problems for women. These are: Anorgasmia, Vaginismus, and Dysparenuia.

Anorgasmia is a difficulty in getting an orgasm.

There are two types of Anorgasmia. There's primary anorgasmia which is where a woman has never been able to reach an orgasm. There's also secondary anorgasmia which is where a woman has been able to have an orgasm in the past but can't seem to any more.

Vaginismus is where the muscles in or around the vagina go into spasm during sex, making sexual intercourse painful, difficult or impossible. For obvious reasons Vaginismus can be very frustrating, upsetting and distressing.

Because muscle spasms are subject to subconscious control, psychological interventions can be very successful indeed. We just need to remove any reason for the subconscious muscle action in order to solve the problem.

Dyspareunia is pain during or after sexual intercourse. It can affect men, but is far more common in women.

Obviously painful intercourse can make sex much less appealing than it would be otherwise. It can affect the way a woman feels about herself, impact on relationships but also, if a woman is trying to get pregnant, then any of these three problems are far from ideal.

In some ways these three problems can be treated in very similar ways and that's why I've introduced them together. Doctors like to give things names of course and to classify things but the names generally aren't helpful. For one thing as soon as something is labelled by a doctor, the expectations which are sometimes created can make it even worse.

So, let's forget about labels for a moment because what we're actually talking about here is essentially the same thing. All these three problems result in difficulty having sex and achieving an orgasm. The exact symptoms are different but to a great extent the result is the same.

Nature has designed the female body to be able to experience orgasms and to enjoy sex in comfort and without pain. Your body is designed to enjoy sex but let's suppose there's been a problem in that regard.

If you have any of the above symptoms then a visit to the doctor should be your first port of call. If there is a physical reason then it needs to be identified and a doctor is most likely to be able to do that.

But, let's suppose there's no obvious physical reason and yet the problem exists. Under those circumstances then you should look to subconscious causes.

If sex has been unpleasantly painful, either regularly, or on occasions, that's not likely to have made you very keen to experience even more of it. There may even be a fear that it will hurt, if it has in the past.

Fear, anxiety and worries tend to make us tense. When people are tense they tend to clench their muscles. You'll have seen people clench their fists or hands when they're anxious. In fact when tense or worried any muscle can clench and tighten and this also applies to muscles in and around the vagina.

Simply having had problems in the past can create a fear and expectation of problems in the future and this is more than enough to cause involuntary clenching in some women, and once again sex is unlikely to be relaxing or enjoyable if that happens.

For a moment imagine a very fortunate woman who has only ever experienced blissful pleasure when having intercourse.

She's had lots of lovely sex with no problems, just lots of pleasure. Because of her experience, this lucky lady has no anxiety and she expects it to be really good. She's got no anxiety so she's got no reason to tense her muscles and she'll have a great time.

So if you have had problems with sex and if it has been painful then a good first step is to get rid of any anxiety. Anxiety isn't helpful because it creates tension so it makes sense to get rid of it.

Fortunately the PSTEC Click Track can easily remove almost all fears and anxieties.

First, using a scale of 0 to 10, rate your fear of sex being painful. Then start the Click Track and follow the instructions. As the track plays, imagine sex being uncomfortable or painful. Try to feel fear and anxiety about that and follow the tapping sequence. After just one or two plays there should be no anxiety left.

This will allow you to have sex without fear of pain and simply by doing this you are far more likely to have a good experience. Certainly you won't clench because of fear.

After getting rid of anxiety regarding pain during sex, the thing to do is to then create the expectation that there won't be any discomfort either.

This will make you far more like the woman in our example who has never had problems at all and who simply expects sex just to be enjoyable, so it is.

You can use suggestion to create a different reaction and expectation. PSTEC Positive is the track you can use to deliver a suggestion to your subconscious to follow. So use PSTEC Positive to tell yourself that you can and will enjoy sex and all will go well.

A good suggestion to use here is as follows:

*When I have sex I will relax and enjoy it*

There's more to do on top of this though. If all the medical reasons for Anorgasmia, Vaginismus, or Dysparenuia have been investigated and eliminated, then the cause is almost always going to be psychological and most likely subconscious.

For this reason, you should remove every possible reason the subconscious may have found for making sex difficult, awkward or even painful. This means that you should remove those reasons. To do this, see the advice contained in the section "Common Causes of Sexual Problems."

# Sexual Jealousy

Jealousy can cause real problems in a relationship. Sometimes people can be jealous about people they have never even met or even imaginary people. It's not uncommon for people to be jealous about their partners past sexual encounters and some people struggle very hard to rid themselves of those feelings. Such feelings are far from ideal. They can poison a relationship, cause anger and arguments and also create suspicion and none of these things are healthy.

Fortunately, in most instances the PSTEC Click Tracks will clear jealousy in minutes. And after the Click Track has removed jealousy regarding their past sexual history, it will almost always stay gone. This is especially true if you then also give yourself a PSTEC Positive suggestion to the effect that you feel absolutely fine about it now.

Some people make the mistake of vividly imagining their partner having graphic sex and then Click Tracking that. It's not the best approach in this instance. Firstly there is no benefit to be had by doing that or by making it sexually graphic. Also, when you do use the Click Track to deal with the jealousy aspect, you don't want to inadvertently hit any of your own excitement connected to the sexual act itself. This is because you also don't want to reduce any of your own desire for your partner. If you inadvertently did that then you'd subsequently have to work on your beliefs related to desire in order to rebuild it.

Here's the correct approach:
The very best way to deal with sexual jealousy is to keep the sex part out of it completely. This may seem surprising but in reality the jealousy will relate to them being with another person. For your subconscious, jealousy is not mostly about sex.

This means that all you should do is to imagine them being emotionally close with that other person (or people) and NOT to imagine it in a sexual context. Try very hard to feel jealous as you do this and Click Track that. If there is anger or some other negative emotion attached then the same approach applies. It may be that you will have to work through anger and jealousy for example.

If the jealousy relates specifically to someone or something in the past then it's a sure sign of your own insecurities. If this is the case it means that you need to work on your own feelings of self-worth. Your own feelings of self-worth are somewhat outside the scope of this book but at the very least, remember that Click Tracks can be applied to negative feelings regarding self. If you have low self-worth and this is a real issue for you then I strongly suggest that you download the PSTEC Level 1 and work through the detailed instructions which specify a systemic approach to self-help.

PSTEC Level 1 is available at www.pstec.org
(Also see the section on Self-image)

# Incompatible Libidos

Sex drives (libidos) can vary wildly and in exactly the same way that sexual jealousy can cause problems in a relationship, very different libidos can cause problems too.

Sometimes couples deal with this by loosening the rules attached to the relationship but it would be a better solution to have both partners' libidos at about the same level.

Sex drives vary between people and can also change within one person dependent upon age, time of day, workload, stress, location, etc.

When libidos are very out of sync, typically one partner will feel frustrated and another may feel inadequate. This can lead to bad temper, ill-chosen words, anger, resentment, etc. It might even lead to a partner looking outside the relationship for the fulfilment they believe they need.

Typically the problems related to "incompatible" libidos will be mostly emotional and it's important to recognise that those emotions actually stem from beliefs. Any thought or self-talk which begins with the words "I need..." is a belief!

There are two approaches here that can work. One is to decrease the high sexual libido in the partner who has a high sex drive. The other is to increase the low sexual libido in the person who has a lower sex drive.

Sex drive should not be Click Tracked unless dealing with something such as Nymphomania or a full blown sex addiction. (See the specific section on that if appropriate)

If you simply want to be more compatible in terms of libido with your partner and the difference is not vast, sex drive can be safely lowered by using PSTEC Positive to directly suggest it. Remember that PSTEC Positive allows you to deliver a suggestion of choice to your subconscious.

The exact choice of words is best if it is yours because it needs to resonate with you but here are some PSTEC Positive suggestions to get you started.


*I'm happy to wait until (name) is ready*
*If I have to wait it will be even better*
*I don't need sex as much as I thought I did*


You'll notice that two of these suggestions make no mention whatsoever of sex. Your subconscious will understand the specific intent as long as you think about sex with your partner BEFORE using the track. You can also think about it as you use the track of course, as per the instructions. This mental focus sets the context into which the subconscious can apply the verbal instruction.

If a libido is low then it might well be increased by directly suggesting it using PSTEC Positive. Before using PTEC Positive in this way for a low libido you should first eliminate all the common causes of sexual problems because they can cause a low libido.
(See "Common Causes of Sexual Problems")

Let's assume that you have already dealt with those. If you also need to use suggestion to increase your libido here are some examples of PSTEC Positive statements that you can use.


*I want sex more*
*I want more sex*
*I love the way sex feels*
*Sex excites me!*
*I want sexual stimulation every day*

You can be much more explicit and graphic with your suggestions if you want to be. This is because you want the suggestion you use to be one that resonates with you emotionally.

Low libido can also be caused by the following:

- Stress,
- Anxiety,
- Depression,
- Feelings of low self-worth and a poor self-image

Stress affects people on a massive scale but often has relatively simple solutions.
(See the section on Stress for some of them)

With regard to anxiety and depression the free PSTEC Therapy system provides the means to deal with much of this by use of the Click Tracks. Remember that you can use them to neutralise unwanted emotions. PSTEC Level 1 provides lots of detail on how to deal with such things. Also check out the free PSTEC interviews.

Self-image can be a significant factor in terms of libido. (If self-image is poor then you should refer to the section on Self-image)

There are also some common physical factors that can cause low libido. Here are a few of the commonest:

- Being overweight tends to lower libido.
- Tobacco smoking is widely thought to adversely affect libido.

If you have really struggled with either of these things you may be interested to know that there are optional and extremely powerful self-help systems for dealing with both of those particular problems on the PSTEC website.

There is a PSTEC Stop Smoking system based on my many years working as a hypnotherapist. There is also a very effective PSTEC weight loss system. And there is also an extremely powerful tool for breaking any food compulsions to junk foods which I suggest you use in combination. All are available on the PSTEC Website.

Some drugs and medications can affect libido.
Significant hormonal changes can affect libido.

Because ill health and physical changes commonly result in an effect on libido, any significant and unexpected change in libido may warrant a trip to see your doctor unless you know the reason for it.

# Nymphomania and Sex Addiction

This particular problem is very often (but not always) related to feelings of insecurity and low self-worth. Sex addiction can be little different from an addiction to drugs or alcohol. People use drugs and alcohol to change their internal state and people sometimes use sex in the same way and for the same reasons. Unlike drugs and alcohol, sex is also often used as a means to get some kind of personal validation. In many ways sex addiction or nymphomania is often not a sexual problem at all. It may be a problem which relates mostly to feelings of low self-worth. For this reason some people even use sex as a kind of self-abuse even though they may not rush to admit it to themselves.

If you've used the free PSTEC Click Tracks then you will probably realise that you can use the Click Tracks on negative feelings regarding self. Click Tracks will lower those negative feelings and this is why it's an important step.

It's possible that simply by doing this it will help long term, but it's more likely to offer a temporary relief only. This is because those feelings are likely to be based on a negative set of beliefs and a very bad habit of negative self-talk so you will need to make a conscious decision to shift the beliefs you have about yourself in a more positive direction.

If you need to deal with negative beliefs regarding self then PSTEC Positive is likely to be very useful to you. As I said earlier, you could also use affirmations but the results would be much, much slower than using the PSTEC tools.
(For more information on this see the following sections: Beliefs, Expectations and Self-image)

If you have an essentially positive self-image but sex addiction is still very much a problem then the approach is different. Under these circumstances it needs to be treated much as I would treat most other behavioural addictions. In order to lower your feelings towards sex, you would imagine the biggest and most inappropriate "turn on" and use a PSTEC Click Track on it. As you do this you will need to try to feel excited throughout. Before doing this be sure that you understand how to use the Click Track and test it on something completely different first. Only use it in the manner just described after you are absolutely sure you are using it correctly and that it works for you.

Whenever Click Tracking sexual excitement you should be prepared to stop the track part way in order to check your level of feeling. This is because you want to lower it, but not completely of course. When using Click Tracks in this way, try ONLY to imagine sexual encounters with strangers and also in the kinds of locations where things have happened before that you would want to avoid in future. If there are any such events in your past about which you feel particularly ashamed, which were dangerous, very stupid or downright nasty then they make ideal candidates for this procedure.

Be sure to recall that event and TRY hard to feel ONLY excitement as you use the PSTEC Click Track on it. Doing this should interrupt your addiction significantly.

Whatever the result, wait a few days and monitor the effect. You can repeat this if necessary.

The following is unlikely but I include this just for the sake of completeness:
If having done this you find it has inadvertently lowered your libido to a level which seems too low then be aware that you can reset it to a higher level by using PSTEC Positive. (See the section on incompatible libidos for details) If however you have been prone to sex addiction you would be well advised to wait a few weeks before doing this. This is because your libido is likely to naturally elevate to a more normal level in that time. Ideally you want to wait for that to happen before introducing another change.

By using the PSTEC tools in the above manner and by also using appropriate self-talk you will find that you can actually exert significant levels of control over your libido.

Be sure also to work through ALL the common causes of sexual problems (see specific section on that) because those things can sometimes have had unexpected effects.

# Premature Ejaculation

Men don't boast about premature ejaculation, but in reality premature ejaculation is not that uncommon and most men will experience it at some time or other. This is a sexual problem which for some men at least leaves them feeling worthless and humiliated. It can be frustrating for both partners.

And so, despite this being less than unusual some men really beat themselves up about their "staying power". And it's something they tend to keep secret which in itself is not good of course because other men are likely to think they are unusual when in reality they are not.

If it's a problem, then there are a few possible solutions. All of the following suggestions are likely to improve the situation significantly.

Let's look at a common but fairly lousy solution first. I do need to say at the outset that this is NOT a solution I would advise.

Some men try to lessen their excitement during intercourse by using a distracting thought which is not sexual in any way. Absolutely, this method might work a little but really who wants to have sex while also trying to work out what kind of glue they use to make cardboard boxes or what colour to paint the garden shed?  If you're a man and you've had problems with premature ejaculation it's possible that you've already tried something along these lines.

In looking for a better solution the place to start is with the mechanics of sexual intercourse. The first and often very practical solution involves a change in position. Different positions will very often bring different outcomes and it can be interesting to experiment anyway.

If premature ejaculation has been a problem for you and you want to last longer than the missionary position is almost certainly a poor choice. In fact, from a staying power perspective the missionary position is one of the very worst positions that you could choose, so try a few others and see what happens.

You're likely to last longer if you're not the one doing the moving. Woman on top provides you with the option to relax and stay still and last longer.

Sex with a condom is also likely to improve the situation. You're likely to last longer wearing a condom than you are without because the stimulation is less direct.

There are muscular exercises that you can do too.
Within the penis there's a muscle which many men say can provide greater control over ejaculation. And like most other muscles it can be strengthened by means of exercise. This is the same muscle that holds your urine from flowing when you need to go to the loo (Note for USA readers. Loo = restroom). The recommended procedure is that over a period of weeks you regularly and deliberately hold the muscle for a while so as to strengthen it. Then when having sex and just before ejaculation you withdraw slightly and hold the muscle.

So there are instant things you can do and also something that requires a bit of practice. What about PSTEC and your subconscious? Does PSTEC provide the means to any other solutions? Yes absolutely because your physical sensitivity, arousal, and also duration are things over which you can exert some control by means of suggestions to your subconscious. Remember that your subconscious exerts a powerful influence over your physiology.

Before doing this though you should use the PSTEC Click Tracks on any frustration if it exists. To do this, think only about premature ejaculation and try only to feel frustration as you run the Click Track and follow the tapping sequences.
Be sure NOT to use the Click Tracks on any other aspect of sex.

Reducing the frustration is an important step because frustration adversely affects your ability to work on expectations and beliefs.

The reality is that where a man genuinely expects to climax very quickly, his subconscious will happily oblige. Similarly the opposite is generally true. Where someone has the genuine expectation that they can last a long time before climaxing then that is far more likely to be the case.

By reducing feelings of frustration you will find it easier to change your expectations and beliefs. Genuinely expecting to last longer each time, is likely to produce a very positive result because your subconscious has so much control over your physiology and physical responses.

Your purpose in lowering any feelings of frustration with Click Tracks is threefold.

- You lower frustration to make you feel happier and more relaxed
- You lower frustration  to allow changes in belief and expectation to be created more effectively
- You also lower frustration because frustration about anything goes hand in hand with doubt

Please remember that when it comes to expectations and beliefs there are some key considerations. (See the sections on Expectation and Belief)

Some suggested PSTEC Positive statements include:

*It's possible to control ejaculations*
*Every time I have sex I expect to last longer*
*I can think in ways to slow down*
*Each time I ejaculate it will take longer to get there*
*I slow sex down to last longer*

These PSTEC Positive suggestions are used to programme your subconscious for change. I suggest using all of the above in sequence.

By doing all of the above you should feel happier and be able to respond differently and you will slow the time it takes to reach climax and ejaculate.

Do not underestimate the power of your own expectations. They play a key role in the way your body responds.

# Abortions

If you have ever had an abortion then the psychological fallout is likely to have been significant. Abortions create all manner of problems for women, sexual and otherwise. The emotional scars from having had an abortion often run very deep. I know from my work as a therapist that abortions and the feelings connected with them rumble on in huge numbers of women for decades.

Such strong and almost entirely negative emotions can cause all manner of problems so they are always best resolved. Typical feelings are guilt, shame and anger. There is no benefit to having those feelings because you already have the knowledge that you learned as a consequence of what happened.

If any of those emotions exist then I strongly suggest that you should clear them with the PSTEC Click Tracks.
Clearance can often resolve sexual problems and also many other things which may not obviously be connected.

After doing any clearance with the Click Tracks I advise using PSTEC Positive with the following suggestions:

*I did my best under the circumstances*
*I forgive myself*

This is because self-forgiveness is an important aspect of letting any guilt go.

# Miscarriages

The feelings connected with miscarriages should always be cleared. The emotional effects of miscarriages have caused more than one sexual problem that I am aware of in my own clients. In ways similar to abortions the effects of things such as guilt can be quite diverse. There is no reason to carry negative emotions so make use of the PSTEC Click Tracks to clear those emotions. The benefits of doing so can be quite unexpected. Certainly if you are trying to get pregnant then clearing any negative emotions regarding past or imagined miscarriages is something I strongly advise.

# Getting Pregnant

Many women would love to have a child but may have struggled to get pregnant and very often the reasons for having had difficulties are not immediately obvious.

It's been widely recognised by knowledgeable hypnotherapy experts that sometimes the subconscious mind has interfered (in various ways) to reduce the chances of a woman conceiving. It's also not unheard of for menstruation to have been similarly affected. In fact The World famous hypnotherapist Dave Elman spoke about this at some length more than sixty years or so ago.

When it comes to fertility, an appropriate use of suggestion is likely to help a great deal. It's important that your self-talk should be genuinely positive because it powerfully affects your expectations and genuine expectations carry far more significance than most people realise.

It's also very important to get your subconscious fully "on-board" with the whole concept of you getting pregnant. This is because your subconscious has so much influence over your physiology.

There are two steps really. The first is to remove any potential subconscious barriers. The second is to provide it with encouragement.

If there are no suspected problems conceiving then I suggest that you do not interfere. The following applies only if problems have been encountered.

In order to stand the very best chance of having a baby it's best to remove any possible reason for your subconscious to interfere. You want your subconscious to work with you towards that wonderful goal.

The first thing to do is to make sure that you have dealt with any previous abortions or miscarriages. (See the preceding sections on how to deal with these)

Next, look at the list of common causes for sexual problems which you'll find earlier in this book. (See section on Common Causes of Sexual Problems)
If any of those common causes apply to you then use the PSTEC tools as explained in order to correct every one of them that might have been affecting you. By eliminating them you will ensure that they have been dealt with and cannot cause problems. This is a very simple and effective way to maximise your chances of conceiving. Remove any and every reason not to.
Another important thing you can do of course is to use the PSTEC Click Tracks to clear any and all frustration about not having managed to conceive yet.

Frustration about conception can cause massive stress. You almost certainly know that already. Well that stress is not conducive to conceiving. This is one reason why I always suggest that you use the PSTEC Click Tracks to clear the frustration. Once you lower the level of frustration with Click Tracks it will leave you feeling less stressed, more relaxed, better able to enjoy sex and also well placed to work on positive expectations.

PSTEC Positive can be used to programme your subconscious for success in getting pregnant and the best way to do this is to use it to work on your expectations.

A positive expectancy gives you a far greater chance of success than a negative one.
Clearing any feelings of frustration needs to be done if any arises because that clears the way for more positive expectations.
(Please see the sections on beliefs, expectations and also PSTEC Positive.)

Add all the positive expectancy you can and then add more! You simply can't overdo it when it comes to expectancy. You can do this with appropriate self-talk. You can also use PSTEC Positive to directly suggest it.

Some particularly good PSTEC Positive statements are:

*I can increase my fertility*
*My fertility is increasing*
*I can be a great parent*
*Children are a joy*
*I can easily become pregnant*
*Everything will go well*
*I'm feeling happy about things*

It is very well known that physical or emotional stress is not helpful when trying to get pregnant. For this reason I advise a couple of other things as being very good ideas. I suggest that you use "PSTEC for Stress in the Moment". That particular PSTEC audio is hugely powerful and is designed to allow you to automatically switch off stress in your mind. The benefit of using it is that it primes your subconscious ready to deal with unexpected stresses. As such it is a perfect tool to use when looking to get pregnant.

If you're eating habits are poor and you find yourself habitually eating junk foods then you may wish to consider the PSTEC tracks for eliminating compulsions to eat sugary, fatty or otherwise junk foods and drinks. It is an absolute certainty that good healthy eating habits will maximise your chances of getting pregnant.

You will find the Food and Drink Compulsion Breakers on the PSTEC website. These particular tracks have been reported as being almost magical in their effects.

After having used these tracks, someone told me yesterday that if they only ever bought one item in their entire lives it would be the PSTEC Food and Drink Compulsion Breakers after learning how effective they are. The results are generally jaw dropping. If you want to have a good healthy diet then those tracks should help you significantly.

If you smoke, bear in mind that it affects fertility. Stopping smoking can be hard unless you go about it in the right way. Fortunately PSTEC also has a self-help system for this and it does work extremely well for most people.

By doing all of the above you should stand a very, very good chance of conceiving.

In about 9 months' time remember to send me an email to let me know your good news.

(Also see the section on Stress)

# Erectile Dysfunction

Many men experience erection problems at some stage. If you've had this problem you're not alone. Erection problems are thought to affect approximately 40% of men by the age of 40, and up to 70% of men by age 70. Viagra and other similar substances have been popular for this very reason.

Before rushing out to order your little blue pills over the Internet you should first see a doctor. Erectile dysfunction can be an early warning of poor health, clogged arteries and serious heart problems.

In fact serious cardiac problems including heart attacks frequently occur three or four years after erectile dysfunction began warning of an impending problem. If you're smart enough to do something about it, then erectile problems may actually prove to be a lifesaver.

A change in lifestyle and eating habits is likely to help greatly and it may also stave off other serious illnesses such as diabetes. Research has shown that improved eating habits and regular exercise can actually reverse the build-up of plaque in the arteries. A 2004 study of obese men with erectile dysfunction found that those who lost about 30 pounds stood a good chance of reversing their erectile problems. Afterwards they were also much less likely to suffer serious illness.

With this in mind it's tragic that so many men think only of the drug approach and fail to discuss things with their doctor. Please bear in mind that whilst drugs for erectile dysfunction work well, they are not without their problems. Almost without exception they do not address the cause.

Here's the stark reality so pay attention. If the problem is caused by clogging of the arteries then taking medication may well improve your sexual prowess in the short term... but sadly that will be of little use to you in the emergency room after a heart attack.

Additionally, drugs for erectile problems are not successful for all men and many men suffer unwanted side effects with the various medications. Headaches are commonly reported and this is not surprising at all, given how the drugs function.

For men who are prepared to use one, a vacuum penis pump is another very reliable answer and unlike medication it has no side effects whatsoever. Once again this should probably be looked on as temporary because if there are arterial problems, then weight loss and a change of lifestyle is essential for your health and long term prospects of not dropping dead.

If you want to lose weight PSTEC offers a wide variety of tools. There is the PSTEC weight loss system. There is a very powerful aid to fasting if you decide to lose weight that way. And the PSTEC food compulsion tracks are almost miraculous in the way they work for most people.

All of these are available at:
www.pstec.org and www.pstecaudiosource.org

You can also use affirmations, positive self-talk and PSTEC Positive to change your attitudes towards exercise and weight loss.
(See sections on beliefs and also on PSTEC Positive)

Smoking can also cause erectile dysfunction.

To get an erection the blood supply must be able to flow freely to and within the penis. But smoking causes hardening of the arteries and blood vessels. As elasticity of blood vessels decreases, so does the flow of blood to the penis. As blood vessels harden, erection problems commonly occur. Hardening of the arteries caused by smoking does cause erectile problems.
To make matters worse for the smokers, nicotine and carbon monoxide also increase blood pressure. And high blood pressure has also been linked to erectile dysfunction in men.

The reality is that if you smoke, then your sex life is likely to suffer and the problems will get worse over time. If you suffer from erectile dysfunction then you need to stop smoking now because it certainly won't be helping. Once again PSTEC comes to the rescue because there is a self-help stop smoking system. If you're going to use it then it may be helpful to know that as a hypnotherapist I worked for a year doing little else but helping people stop smoking. My success rate was so high that I was able to offer a "no win, no fee" arrangement to my clients. The PSTEC self-help system for stopping smoking is based on what I was doing way back then that proved so successful.

The PSTEC system for smokers has even more power, so you can be optimistic.

So far we've talked about losing weight and stopping smoking in order to correct erectile problems. What pleasures will be left in life for you? Well, how about you live long enough to enjoy a great sex life? Everything has an upside ... In this case, literally.

Obviously not all erection problems are caused by physical factors. Very often erectile problems can occur as a result of what's going on in your subconscious.

A wide variety of emotional and psychological factors can affect a man's ability to get an erection.

Do any of these typical psychological causes apply to you?

- Stress and anxiety (from work or home)
- Problems within the relationship
- Worrying about pleasing a sexual partner
- Fear of intimacy
- Fears about consequences becoming a father
- Beliefs about sex and early life programming
- Guilt
- Fears of contracting sexually transmitted diseases
- Frustration
- Alcohol problems
- Depression

For Stress and anxiety (from work or home) you can use the free
PSTEC Click Tracks. If you have other PSTEC tools such as Level 1
or the Accelerators, then you can use those too of course. If you're
going through something of a difficult time then regular use of
"PSTEC for Stress in the Moment" can be a good idea too.
(See the section on Stress for more information)

Problems within the relationship are covered at some length in
PSTEC Level 1. If you haven't got that then you can at least use the
free Click Tracks to remove many or all of your negative feelings.

Worrying about pleasing a sexual partner is best addressed by looking
at your beliefs rather than Click Tracking. In fact I'd generally advise
against that unless you do it the following way. Imagine your partner
being cross with you for failing to perform sexually. Try to feel
anxious as you imagine this and Click Track that.

Fear of intimacy. Fear of intimacy is generally connected to feelings
of self-worth. There may be a body dysmorphia element too. The
simplest method of using PSTEC to deal with this is to identify the
things about yourself that have caused you concern, and try very hard
to feel anxious about them as you run the Click Tracks.
If you want to increase your confidence in a more general sense then
also refer to the section on Self-image.

Fears of becoming a father can be Click Tracked. Simply imagine
being a father and use PSTEC Click Tracks to eliminate the fear.

Similarly, guilt is also easily addressed by using the free PSTEC Click
Tracks or similar. (EEfs or Accelerators)

If your fears are of contracting a sexually transmitted disease then
you can Click Track that fear. Obviously you should then take steps
to always have sex safely.

Frustration is usually easy to remove with PSTEC Click Tracks. This
is a good idea and an important step because frustration and negative
expectations very often go hand in hand. Just eliminating feelings of

frustration will leave you feeling more relaxed and more likely to get an erection when aroused.

Alcohol problems and depression can both be dealt with by using the PSTEC tools. The various tutorials and also the free interviews should be consulted if either of these is a factor for you.

If you were brought up with beliefs that have caused you problems engaging in sex then you will need to change those beliefs. One of the best ways to counter your early programming is to deliberately look for counter examples. Counter examples are anything you can identify in the world which totally contradicts what you were taught. Consciously looking for counter examples can be a powerful method of personal change. You can back it up with self-talk or preferably PSTEC Positive.

(Also see the following sections, Stress, Common Causes of Sexual Problems, PSTEC Tools, Beliefs, Expectations)

# Erotic Asphyxiation

Thousands of people die every year because of this highly dangerous sexual habit. Many people who continue to do this are absolutely terrified that their habit will kill them and yet they continue because they feel a compulsion.

If you have this problem and you're reading this then you almost certainly want to stop but the attraction has been so powerful that you've continued.

Like many aspects connected to sex this might feel like an addiction but it's actually only a behavioural compulsion. This distinction means it should be easy for you to resolve as long as you use PSTEC.

Some people feel disgusted with themselves for having this habit, but let me give you a different perspective. People have always sought thrills in a multitude of ways. This is why roller coaster rides and other similar entertainments are so popular. Those things are regarded as being perfectly normal. If erotic asphyxiation was safe there'd be no problem but it's not. It's highly dangerous and potentially lethal. You can rest assured that amongst the many thousands of people who have died already, almost all were kidding themselves that they'd be okay.

Here's the procedure for correcting this:
Get your choice of Click Track ready to play. And then imagine that you're just about to do some erotic asphyxiation.

Rate the feeling of excitement that you can get from that thought on a scale of zero to ten and then begin a Click Track.

1. Keep imagining the experience of having that bag over your head.
2. Try as hard as you can to feel thrilled and excited and try really hard to hold that emotion throughout the duration of the track as it plays.

3. Follow the tapping sequence.

Repeat until the feeling drops down to a one or a zero.

Then use your choice of PSTEC Positive track with the following suggestion:

*I must have been an idiot*

This suggestion will not sit comfortably with some readers. That's exactly the point. The bottom line is that this emotive suggestion will help your subconscious to protect you.

This simple procedure may require some repetition but it should resolve the problem.

# Swinging and Dogging

(Also see the section on Nymphomania and Sex Addiction)

Many people who engage in certain types of sexual activity do so because it suits them and they enjoy it. If you're happy with your lifestyle and you're sure you're not hurting anyone else then there should be no problem.

Other people who find themselves drawn to swinging and dogging really hate themselves for doing it and those people need solutions.

If you're regularly doing something which makes you unhappy then you need to look at why. Is it happening because of a self-image problem?

Sometimes people who have low feelings of self-worth end up engaging in sexual activity as a sort of escape. Unfortunately when people engage in sex for the wrong reasons it generally makes them feel even worse about themselves. This can end up in a cycle of sexual activity which continually provides the occasional release but which ultimately makes someone feel much, much worse.

If this is the case then the starting point for a solution is to work on your feelings of self.
(See the section on Self-image)

Another thing that you can do is change your emotional response to the things you've found yourself doing.

As human beings we are full of conflicts and very often people continue to do something which one part of them wants to do but another part doesn't.

Let's suppose that someone regularly finds themselves engaging in group sex. They do it perhaps because of the physical sensations and the thrill they get from it. Also they are getting some attention. But at exactly the same time, that same person may feel totally disgusted with themselves and feel awful about what they've been doing. Conflicting emotions, beliefs and behaviours are very common in people and they cause endless problems.

The way to deal with this is deal with two things. You will need to look at self-image (see above) and also to deal directly with the sexual activity itself.

With regard to the latter you identify the aspect which causes the most disgust in you and then use the PSTEC Click Tracks in the following way:

Vividly imagine the thing that you have been doing sexually and make it extreme. Be sure to include the location and context. As the Click Track plays follow the tapping sequences and try very hard to feel sexual excitement throughout the track.
Use the Click Track to lower your emotional feelings about it. Use the track until the excitement regarding that scenario is lower.

Be sure to Click Track ONLY those things which you want to avoid and not to feel excited by. Frequently and carefully check your progress as you proceed. Immediately afterwards use these two PSTEC Positive statements:

*I hated doing that*
*I still really love sex though*

Leave it a few days or weeks and monitor the effects. If you need to repeat the procedure you can.
Be sure to also work on your self-image. (See the section on Self-image)

Once your sexual activity has normalised to a level which makes you happier then you should also use Click Tracks to eliminate any guilt regarding what you were doing. Immediately after this I suggest PSTEC Positive with suggestions along the following lines:

*Everyone makes mistakes sometimes*
*Now my life will be better*

# Internet Porn Addiction

With the arrival of telecommunications and the mass media pornographers have proliferated like never before. This proliferation illustrates very clearly that a fundamental aspect of humanity is that of sexuality, and addiction to pornography seems to be on the increase.

In many ways an addiction to pornography can be dealt with rather like the method described for swinging and dogging. You can use a PSTEC Click Track on those feelings of compulsion but if you do then you need to do it in the right way.

In this instance I suggest that you use PSTEC Positive first. Remember, you can use PSTEC Positive to give yourself and your subconscious suggestions of change.

I suggest working through all the following PSTEC Positive statements:

*Porn is horrible*
*Porn is unpleasant*
*Porn exploits people*
*Porn is for losers*
*I'm finished with that*
*I'd rather do other things*

If you have a hobby then I also suggest using the following:

*(Name of hobby or interest) is much more interesting*

The above should be worked through one after another for a few days. All of the above should be done in sequence each time.

Next monitor what happens for a while. If your interest wanes which is very likely, then there should be little more to do. If it does not then you will need to directly reduce the emotions connected with viewing porn.

If that is the case then the procedure is as follows:

Get some porn handy of the kind you've been viewing. Make sure it's of the kind that disgusts you at some level but which has attracted you at another. Obviously make sure it's legal to view and when Click Tracking such things I strongly advise you to stick to the kinds of things that you'd be very reluctant to do personally. If that's not possible then use some of the more extreme examples of the kind of things you've been viewing. This means that as you reduce your interest in these with a Click Track it is unlikely to affect your default sex drive.

With those images very fresh in your mind, immediately turn off the computer or close the magazine and run the PSTEC Click Track straight away in the following manner...

Imagine those images vividly in your mind and stay focussed on them as the track plays. TRY hard to feel excitement throughout and follow the tapping sequence. This will direct your subconscious to remove or significantly lower any feelings of excitement attached to such images.

Because you don't want to affect other aspects of your sexuality I also advise a little by little approach with this. Be prepared to stop the track part way and assess your feelings every now and again.

Once the problem is thoroughly resolved, make a conscious decision that you'll not bother to look at these things again and then don't.

If you're in a relationship and you became addicted to porn then there is also likely to be some guilt attached.

Some people choose not to Click Track their guilt because they feel it makes them less likely to do the same things again.

My personal opinion is the opposite. Guilt has the tendency to make you think about what caused the guilt in the first place and that's not what you want if at some point you had an "addiction," behavioural or otherwise.

As long as you have the knowledge that you don't want to go back, then you can safely remove any guilt and it's better to do so. Guilt is something that you should easily be able to remove with PSTEC Click Tracks.

# Male Orgasmic Disorder

Male orgasmic disorder is where everything goes to plan in the early stages of a sexual encounter, with an erection and arousal, but then the man is unable to achieve an orgasm. Male orgasmic disorder can be caused by many things, surgery being one of them. If you have had a prostatectomy then that could be a cause and if you have had such an operation you will need to talk to your doctor if male orgasmic disorder is a problem.

Psychological factors are also very common causes. The two most likely and common psychological causes are stress (mind on other things) and also performance anxiety.

If you think that the problem may be performance anxiety then that can be dealt with by means of the PSTEC Click Tracks and PSTEC Positive.

(See the sections on Premature Ejaculation and Erectile Dysfunction for details)
(See also the section on Stress)

# Illegal or Unusual Attractions and Paraphilias

One of the most astonishingly crazy and truly awful things that I heard recently was of a method that had been tested for the treatment of paedophiles. It was a treatment designed by psychologists who honestly expected it to work, but for me it displays an astonishing lack of knowledge regarding the way people actually function.

Their subjects were apparently made to watch images of children and they were encouraged to masturbate at the same time. Then immediately before they climaxed, pictures of adults were substituted. The psychologists hope was that this would fix the problem. This is a treatment that would NEVER work! Part of me wants to say "shame on the idiots who came up with it" but they were at least trying to find a cure for something which causes untold misery.

Someone cannot help being attracted to certain things but they can certainly make choices about whether they act on those attractions. People become attracted to all manner of things, and the variety of human sexual attractions is truly mind boggling. For some reason psychiatry has wanted to name them all but what a pointless exercise that is and in a moment you'll see why.

I promised not to go into too much detail re theory in this book but here I'm going to because I want you to make sense of this. In essence it's very simple and not mysterious at all.

In Pavlovian conditioning a stimulus becomes neurologically connected to a response. This happens by means of new neural connections being created when things happen at the same time. Repetition or intensity makes them stronger. Pavlov's experimental subjects were dogs and through repetition they connected the idea of a bell ringing to food being delivered.

Have you ever wondered how a person becomes sexually attracted to trees? I suspect not, but some people find them a real "turn on." Other people are sexually attracted to clowns or nuns or horses or any number of other seemingly bizarre and unusual things. This happens by exactly the same process.

You see, if someone is aroused and also happens to be exposed to a particular stimulus at the same time as that arousal occurs then they subconsciously connect the two things together. This happens outside of conscious awareness and is automatic. It does not necessarily cause an attraction and usually it will not, but if repeated sufficiently or potently enough then this unconsciously created connection becomes stronger.

It may reach a point whereby the external stimulus can then trigger a feeling of attraction.

It's by this simple process that some people can initially become attracted to certain things other than those which nature generally intended.

Then it gets more complex because beliefs start to exert some power in the equation too. When someone is old enough to use language in order to think things to themselves people notice that certain things change their arousal state. Usually they will mentally comment on it in their heads and this self-talk is a complex reinforcement of what was a simple neural connection.

Self-talk is actually the most powerful form of suggestion going and at that point it powerfully reinforces what's been inadvertently created. After that if there is any acting out in any way at all it will further reinforce the attraction since both stimulus and response once again get fired off together.

It should not be at all surprising therefore that some people find horses sexually attractive. By the same mechanism they could just as easily be frightened of them and some people are.

Similarly, some people find clowns a genuine turn on. Other people are scared of clowns. Neither makes logical sense to most people but both those instances are the results of similar processes.

On the subject of self-talk I do want to make the following point. Throughout this book I've talked about that and also about the power of suggestion and auto-suggestion (self-talk). As soon as someone starts telling themselves that they are attracted to this or that, then guess what happens? They start to change the way they think and feel about those things.

As an extreme example of the power of words in this context, consider what a stage hypnotist might say to one of his volunteers.

"From this moment that lovely looking chair over there will seem like the most sexually attractive thing in the world and you'll find it really turns you on. Every time you look at it you'll feel more aroused and you'll really want to embrace it passionately...."

This may be only a few words strung together in the form of a suggestion but words have tremendous power. Self-talk certainly does because we tend not to argue with it.

For anyone who doubts the reality of stage hypnosis I can assure you that it's real. What's used? Words. Most people massively underestimate the power that words have to affect us.

Okay, so let's go back to the paraphilias and how to solve them.

For many paraphilias (generally unusual sexual attractions), you need to break the connection between the arousal state and the stimulus to which it became connected.
This means that if you are attracted to something which is out of the ordinary and you want to end that attraction then you end it by using the PSTEC Click Tracks.

The procedure is pretty much the same for all such things so let's use horses as an example. Let's assume that horses really turn you on and you want to change that. Here's what you would do.

When running the PSTEC Click Track you would think vividly about horses (the most sexy and attractive ones). At the same time, and as you think about the sexy horses try very hard to feel aroused throughout the Click Track and also do your best to follow the tapping sequence.

Rate the feeling before and after the Click Track. Then when the feeling is really low you can stop. The attraction to horses should then be gone.

If you want to change your feelings about anything, then you can also use self-talk to do that. Generally PSTEC Click Tracks are the place to begin. Then use your self-talk appropriately to put the problem completely in the past.

# Summary

At some stage I may expand this book to cover even more issues and problems. For now though this will hopefully serve as an indication as to the many ways in which you can use PSTEC tools for sexual problems. If your problem hasn't been specifically covered then by looking at all the information here you should be able to infer a solution.

Many things can be undertaken by using the free system and a bit of suitable self-talk.
Personally I believe that it makes absolute sense to make maximum use of all the PSTEC tools where appropriate simply because that will be the shortest and easiest route to the best and fastest results.

I'm not instructing you to do any of the above because these are exactly the methods I would use with paying clients.

I hope that by reading this book you will now be able to enjoy a happier, and more fulfilling sex life. I also hope that you have learned a lot about PSTEC and its capabilities.

Enjoy your day and a better sex life.

Best Wishes,

Tim Phizackerley

# Legal

Just a quick reminder on a couple of things.

All self-help comes with personal responsibility. This book explains how I would personally undertake to treat or resolve a wide variety of issues. This is not an instruction to do as I would. Ultimately all self-help is a choice. Some issues may be slightly different or have unusual aspects and so my primary aim in writing this is to allow you to understand how PSTEC and the Click Tracks can be used in the context of resolving sexual problems. If in any doubt you should consult a practitioner.

Every user of PSTEC tools should consult the terms of use on www.pstec.org.

Commercial and business use is subject to certain limitations and this is designed to prevent wholesale exploitation of my work by large organisations without credit, so do check out the terms on the website.

# Coming Soon!

In Summer 2014, I expect to be able to release a new core track.

This new tool will sit alongside the Click Tracks and PSTEC Positive at the very heart of the system. It's taken me almost a decade to develop PSTEC to its current level and this new tool will enhance PSTEC massively by opening up entirely new possibilities for fast personal change.

Be sure that everyone you know is on the mailing list because this isn't something to miss.

# Links

After almost ten years of development, PSTEC now offers an array of tremendously powerful tools. Here are some useful links to the resources discussed in this book. There are a couple of other links included that are especially popular. Begin with the free PSTEC system. I advise everyone to use that first and to confirm for themselves that these tools really do work. After you discover that it genuinely does work, there is a whole world of possibility for you to explore.

**The Free PSTEC Self-help System**
http://www.pstec.org  or http://www.pstecaudiosource.org

**Click Tracks Made Simple**
http://www.pstec.org/clicktracksmadesimple.php

**PSTEC Level 1**
http://www.pstec.org/therapists2.php

**The PSTEC users Forum**
http://pstecforum.com/pf/

**PSTEC Positive Secrets**
http://www.pstec.org/pstecpositivesecrets.php

**PSTEC Positive Extra Power**
http://www.pstec.org/pstecpositivesecrets.php

**PSTEC Accelerators**
http://www.pstec.org/accelerators.php

**PSTEC for Stress in the Moment**
http://www.pstec.org/stress-in-the-moment.php

**Stop Smoking Self-help**
http://www.pstec.org/stop-smoking-system.php

**Stop Smoking For Therapists**
http://www.pstec.org/stop-smoking.php?pagefor=therapist

**Weight Loss**
http://www.pstec.org/weight-loss.php

**Food and Drink Compulsion Breakers**
http://www.pstec.org/end-food-addictions.php

**Alternate Day Fasting**
http://www.pstec.org/fasting.php

**How to Achieve Almost Anything - The Easy Way**
http://www.pstec.org/achieve.php

**Interviews with real users of PSTEC**
http://www.pstec.org/talks.php

**Think And Grow Rich With PSTEC**
http://pstecaudiosource.org/think-and-grow-rich-pstec